What Doesn't Kill You...

The Headache from Hell and a Relentless Search for Healing

by Danny Friedman

EMERALD LAKE
BOOKS

Books published by Emerald Lake Books may be ordered through booksellers or by contacting:

Emerald Lake Books
44 Green Pond Rd
Sherman, CT 06784

http://emeraldlakebooks.com
860-946-0544

ISBN: 978-0-692-39736-7

Printed in the United States of America

Danny Friedman is an unstoppable powerhouse of positivity who found himself suddenly...stopped.

Between the pages of this book, his journey of anguish, perseverance, and even (maybe especially) laughter will become a palpable guidepost for you on how to break through the biggest obstacles in your life head first (minus the ache). Every chapter is a chuckle, every lesson practical and vital.

Danny's overcoming story will teach you how to use the grit of tenacity plus the grace of humor to conquer the art of living, a purposeful book suffused with pain, hope, and the freedom that comes in fighting for your own healing.

Bobby Lehew
Chief Branding Officer
ROBYN Promotions

Equal Parts Hysterical and Inspirational! Danny masterfully navigates the world of healthcare in pursuit of a cure for a chronic headache. His search runs the gamut from visits to a high priestess to traditional practitioners. With humor, he leads the reader through his journey while revealing the life tenets that allowed him to persevere in the face of madness. An inspirational read that will incite big laughs!

Chris Vanderzyden
Author of
7 Steps to Entrepreneurial Victory!

A universal tale of the human condition, made special by the inclusion of simple, yet fundamental life lessons. Heads up! Read this now.

Evan D. Rossio
Owner
Rossio Law PLC

Insightful, entertaining and inspiring, Danny weaves valuable insights in a very personal story reminding us all to be mindful of what others may be going through without being preachy. Once I picked it up, I couldn't put it down until it was finished.

Dale T Denham
Chief Information Officer
Geiger

Danny Friedman provides wonderful insights in this very personal medical journey. Through humor and examples he shares a timely narrative for anyone trying to navigate adversity. His words "never ever give up" are woven throughout this remarkable tale and have become his very own words to live by.

Lori Popkewitz Alper
Founder and Editor in Chief
Groovy Green Livin

I can't believe I have known Danny for 23 years. His enthusiasm for life with work, family, friends and life is contagious. This book confirms everything I have known about him: that perseverance and being your own advocate, along with a sense of humor, are essential for everything in life. Bravo, Danny. You are an inspiration.

Dean Salita
Law Partner
Brabbit & Salita, P.A.

If you've met Danny you can literally hear his humor as he relates his journey through and out of a life of pain while learning lessons in humility, courage and perseverance. His story is inspirational.

Laura Forbes
Former President (Retired)
Zebra Marketing

To everyone I love—without them I would not be here today to tell my story—and most of all to Lisa, Sydney and Cameron, who are overwhelmingly the main reason I fought so hard to get well.

Contents

Acknowledgements

I want to acknowledge all of the doctors, therapists and other medical practitioners that cared about me and truly tried to help me solve this unreal mystery.

I thank Chris Vanderzyden for her wisdom and being the driving force that has turned my story into the next chapter of my life. This book wouldn't have happened without her.

I also thank Dr. Bernadette Kohn and Jeannie Browning of the Kohn Medical Group for saving my life. They will never know the true extent of what they actually did. They not only saved my family, but they enabled me to survive this ordeal and pass on my story so that I may help others.

Finally, there are the ladies of "Estrogen Island." Lisa, my best friend and partner in life, whose undying support along with our daughters, Sydney and Cameron, gave me the daily motivation to get better. They had to put up with me at the lowest time of my life and I know that wasn't easy.

And finally, thanks to my friends whose unconditional support kept me going strong and gave me the will to pursue this project.

Foreword

I first met Danny in 1983 when we were both freshman at Ohio State University. We were pledging the same fraternity and building friendships that would last the rest of our lives. There were eight of us, but we weren't just close friends. We were brothers; brothers that would do anything and support any one of the group.

I knew about Danny's chronic daily headaches, but didn't understand the magnitude until 2012 and what it was doing to his life. This was around the two-year mark of his ordeal.

It's not in Danny's DNA to complain and it's for sure not in him to make this health ordeal his identity. As long as I've known him, he's been one of the most upbeat, energetic and positive people around. So this was very disheartening, not only to me, but to the rest of the "Brothers."

Knowing Danny the way I do, I know that, without saying anything, he was leaning on all of us for support. He has told me that the support and love he felt from not only his "brothers," but from everyone else he loved, is the only thing that got him through this.

This self-reflection tells me what kind of person

Danny is. Danny "gets it."

Maybe he "got it" before going through this ordeal, but I know that he now understands *what* is and *who* are important in his life.

This book is a must-read for anyone who is suffering through a health issue, their families dealing with the person suffering, and for anyone going through tough times.

Danny's story is an inspiration to everyone because it tells of a man who never gave up, even when the entire healthcare system failed him.

He learned that with the support of loved ones and the perseverance to keep moving forward no matter what obstacles stand in your way, you can achieve whatever you set out to do and, in turn, we all learn from his story.

Dr. Daniel Erlanger, DO

The Journey Begins

Welcome to the "Shit Happens" Club

My name is Danny Friedman and I've been in sales for 27 years. For the last 18 years, I have been in the promotional products industry (items with corporate logos on them). I'm like all the other Jewish guys in the promo industry who were not smart enough to get into law school or medical school. We became salesmen.

I've worked with Fortune 500 companies and I've been a sales manager and trainer for the last twelve years.

All in all, I'm a pretty normal guy – a suburban Dad. I'm in my 40s, married with two children, and I don't smoke or drink.

For college, I went to Ohio State, and I live and die Ohio State football – I mean, I have issues. I'm sitting in a room right now that is painted scarlet and gray and has Ohio State everything all over it. I'm a crazy Ohio State fan and still friends with eight guys that I was in a fraternity house with. These guys aren't just my friends. They're my brothers.

Ever since I was little, I've always played sports, had a ton of energy and worked out. I wouldn't say I ate the healthiest, and I did my fair share of partying in my day, but I worked out a lot.

These days, I have a funky diet – I call it the "4½ + 2½ diet." From Sunday night to Friday afternoon, I eat healthy foods, such as salads, grilled fish, fruits, vegetables, stuff like that... But from Friday afternoon to Sunday afternoon, I eat like a dumpster fire. I eat whatever I want, however much I want.

I still work out a lot, including playing basketball once a week. I'm 49 years old and have the energy of a 15-year-old.

But one thing that not many people know about me is that I endured a 2½-year health ordeal – something I've kept a secret until now.

In my life, I've known many people (heck, I'm related to a few) that made a health issue their identity.

Not me. No way. No how. It wasn't in my DNA.

I've always been healthy, strong, energetic and had a positive attitude. I kept this a secret because of who I am. I would not show weakness or any flaw in my otherwise upbeat personality.

Like others, I've had the common cold before, but until 2011, I had never experienced anything like this. I had chronic, *daily* headaches, 24 hours a day, for 2½ years straight.

I went through doctors and specialists and

medications with funky side effects. I even took 18 Botox shots to my head. Yeesh!

But nobody could ever figure out what was wrong with me.

Between all the crazy side effects that came with the ridiculous amount of different medications I took, I actually managed to come up with some humorous stories and anecdotes about the whole experience now that I've gotten better.

If you've ever dealt with any kind of adversity, I hope you'll find some inspiration as well as entertainment in this book, *What Doesn't Kill You...*

I learned some major lessons from this experience, and it's my hope that you'll learn them too.

Anyone, no matter who they are, can encounter adversity, but you can't give up, no matter what. You've got to keep fighting because every day is a gift. Enjoy your life as it is today. Don't ever take it for granted because it can change in an instant, never to be the same again.

Homecoming (Or What Happens When Danny Gets Bored)

Recipe for Success! Making Chicken Salad Out of Chicken %*#$#!

Before these headaches took over my life, I couldn't help but think about what my life used to be like. For example, there was this time when one of my daughters went to her Homecoming dance.

The year was 2009, and my daughter was a freshman in high school that year. She had just become friends with a new group of girls. Two things became quickly apparent to me.

The first thing was that most kids these days go to dances like it's fantasy football, picking their teams ahead of time. The boys don't ask out individual girls. Instead, groups are organized, matching up couples with friends helping other friends out. Some of these kids' dates are complete strangers. Go figure...

The second thing was that, in today's world, Homecoming, Prom and Turnabout (Sadie Hawkins Dance for you old folks) have become such over-the-top events that they range from small bar mitzvahs to Princess Diana's wedding... Crazy!

5

What happened to going to the dance and a nice dinner? Not today. Limos, $200 dinners, staying overnight somewhere, and just general over-the-top behavior is the norm.

Okay. Back to my daughter's homecoming. She was with a new group of friends (who she wasn't still friends with two months later) that had figured out this year's Homecoming roster. My daughter was going with a boy she really didn't know, but that's par for the course.

So the weekend arrived and, of course, there was a pre-Homecoming Dance get-together at the house of the Queen Bee of the girls. This gathering was for pictures and hors d'oeuvres.

Basically, it was to document the night via pictures that would be on Facebook three minutes after they were taken to show the world what a great time everyone was having, and how cool everyone is.

My wife and I showed up at this person's house with my wife's famous taco dip (easily the best food item my wife makes, with her banana bread a close second).

We entered this house and it was like a bad business cocktail party. My daughter was hanging with the girls and the boys were all standing in a corner. Meanwhile, my wife and I were making small talk with people we just met. I actually enjoy meeting new people, but these people were *boring*! Brutally boring.

Well... What happens when Danny gets bored? He finds the need to entertain himself and that's usually at the expense of some unsuspecting soul.

So, I began walking around and my opportunity hit me smack in the face.

Most of the parents were in the kitchen and it just so happened that the seven boys of this gala event were standing in the kitchen too. One of the Dads was standing with these seven boys, who were dressed in standard teenage boy dance attire: a light blue Oxford shirt and khaki pants. (Change the shirt to a red polo and they all would look like they worked for OfficeMax).

Heads Up!

In the buffet line of life, you get to fill your own tray. Do you want cold soup and an old bologna sandwich or cookies, cakes and ice cream sundaes? Make every day a dessert!

The Dad standing by these boys was also wearing a light blue Oxford shirt and khaki pants.

This was a layup for me.

Eventually, there was a break in conversation and an awkward silence in the room. I decided to move in for the kill.

I walked up to the Dad and the seven boys and asked, "Hey... Did you guys get a deal at the clothing shop? You buy seven little outfits and get the big one free?"

My wife laughed and the rest of the crowd was dead silent. The Dad I busted on really didn't appreciate being lumped with the fashion style of 14-year-old boys. Tough crowd.

It also probably wasn't good that the guy I goofed on was the father of my daughter's date.

At that point, my wife and I quietly left the house with our taco dip. (No one touched that or any of the food that we were instructed to bring).

It ended up that my daughter had a nice time, while I continued my record-breaking streak of pissing someone off at every social function I attend.

Yeah, You Have an Eye Infection

Can I Please See Some ID?

Until my health issues began, life was normal. I was the "Demented Ward Clever." I was working a regular job, had a wife and two teenage daughters, and that was my life, though always viewed through my humorous and atypical point of view.

Everything was going well and the only health issues I ever had were non-life-threatening surgeries. I had three shoulder surgeries and a knee surgery – all sports-related.

I'm your typical Weekend Warrior+. (The "+" is because I play sports *and* work out weekdays too!)

I always tell people I'm like a great car. I have a great engine, but a bad body that needs occasional repairs.

October is one of my favorite months because of Halloween and Ohio State football games.

One year, I revived a Halloween tradition that I hadn't done in years. It was something that only the Demented Ward Cleaver would do.

I got a scary mask, which got a big thumbs up from my Halloween Advisory Committee (my daughters) and dressed in all black. Then I sat in my driveway with a bowl of candy that had a sign on it that read "PLEASE

9

TAKE ONLY ONE."

I sat there without moving a muscle so the trick-or-treating kids wouldn't know if I was real or fake.

A lot of the kids were freaked out (some adults too) when I made sudden movements. (For example, when I grabbed their hands as they reached into the bowl.) Some kids, as old as 12 or 13, wouldn't even approach me.

I did have one rule: I would not scare any little ones (usually about 4 years or younger). Instead I would say, "Happy Halloween. Want some candy?"

This was for my pure entertainment. My wife and daughters won't admit that they enjoy it, but they always watch from inside and they *do* have fun.

The following episode was the highlight of the day:

[A Dad, a 7-year-old girl and a 5-year-old boy are across the street from me.]

Dad: Hey, guys! There's a skeleton over there. Go check it out.

[The kids cross the street and approach me very cautiously.]

Girl: Dad! It's fake. It's a doll!

[As she's turning to yell to Dad, I slowly turn my head to face the boy.]

Boy: He's real! He's not fake. He just moved!

Girl: No, he didn't move. It's a doll.

Dad [*yells*]: It's fake. Don't worry about it. It's not real.

They go on their way with the little boy pleading his case. So not only didn't they believe him, I'm pretty sure he soiled his Spiderman costume!

I love Halloween!

There's another fall tradition that I look forward to. Every year, my fraternity brothers and I travel to Columbus, Ohio, to see our beloved football team play at least once. I look forward to it every year. We go crazy. We're old farts trying to see if we're still young.

As usual, in October of 2011, we went to a football game at Ohio State. The weather was just terrible (cold and rainy), but I sat through the game for four hours. Ohio State lost, which bummed me out even more. Still, we had a good time.

About two or three weeks after the football game, I got a cold. I don't get colds too often, but I'm the type of person that when I do get a cold, it's not like I just have the sniffles for a few days. My body completely shuts down. That's me, Captain Extreme. I'm always doing things at 150 mph and that includes getting sick.

I suffered through my cold, but eventually it went

away. About a month later, I noticed that my eyes were getting itchy and heavy. It made me stop and think because I had never experienced that before from a cold.

The only issue I've ever had that was related to my eyes was the Lasik surgery I had about 12 years ago. At the time, it was a success, although now I wear glasses because I'm old and I can't see up close.

I've always been a healthy guy, so I wasn't concerned that I wasn't feeling well. It wasn't severe at that point. I just thought I had an eye infection and that it was getting irritated.

Itching eyes weren't normal for me though, so I decided to go to my general physician. He was a newer, kind-of-young nice guy. I just said to him, "I've got these bad itchy eyes."

My doctor checked me out and gave me these words of wisdom, "Take these eye drops."

I figured I'd take the drops for 3 or 4 days and that would be it. I went home, spent time with my family, and went to work just as I would have done normally.

I used the eye drops as directed, but nothing happened. Then I started to feel a pressure in my head. That's when things began to get unusual.

A week after I started taking the eye drops, I went to an eye doctor. This doctor must have been new because he looked like he was about 11 years old, but he was an eye doctor. I didn't know if his diploma was from the University of Grenada, but I trusted him.

He looked at me and said, "Yeah, you have an eye infection."

That's the funny thing... Every doctor, God bless 'em, has an off-the-charts ego. Every single one that I talked to on this journey said with confidence, "Yeah, it's this" or "Yeah, it's that." About 98% of them were wrong.

This guy said, "You've got an eye infection. Let me give you drops."

Well, he gave me drops and, me being a moron and not even checking, I took them. Later I found out that they were the same drops that the general physician had prescribed to me. I didn't even notice because I was preoccupied with getting rid of this "eye infection."

I gave the drops another shot, but they still weren't working.

At this point, I started to feel a lot of pressure in my sinus area, under my cheeks and eyes, and my forehead. A *lot* of pressure. I began to think that that something was seriously wrong.

The Hot Tea Nasal Rinse

If at First You Don't Succeed... You Know the Rest!

About a week after I went to the eye doctor, I went to Doctor #3: an allergist. I had never been to an allergist in my life. Maybe I'm getting old, but she seemed really young, too.

The first thing she said to me was, "You probably have a sinus infection, but let's test you for allergies."

Now this was just one of the many unpleasant procedures that I had to go through in this 2½-year journey. It was very unpleasant. She proceeded to give me ten shots in the arm and thirty pricks with little needles.

I laughed and joked, "30 pricks and 10 shots? It sounds like I'm at a bachelor party."

Luckily, she found it funny. Some of these doctors had no sense of humor. After she ran the tests, she came back to me and said, "You're not allergic to anything."

It seemed that going to all these doctors and taking all these tests only permitted me to find out what I *didn't* have, like I found out I didn't have any allergies.

She said, "You probably have a sinus infection," which, by the way, I'd never had a sinus infection before.

The allergist prescribed me two medications, a Z-Pak

15

antibiotic and Prednisone, which was a steroid – not like the one that would build muscles, but a steroid that would reduce the pressure in my face and head.

She also told me to use a neti pot, which looked like a little plastic tea pot from a kid's tea set. You poured a saline solution into one nostril with the pot and it came out the other nostril. It was really unpleasant. It was like a hot tea nasal rinse. I had to do this twice a day.

So I was on the Z-Pak, Prednisone and rinsing my nose out with tea twice a day. It was a very funky feeling. When the Z-Pak was done, and I still was feeling badly, she prescribed me this other drug called "Augmentin," which, if I am correct, was my fourth medication.

With all the medicines I was prescribed over this journey I could have opened my own pharmacy.

I kept taking all these medications for the entire month. At the end of the month, a pattern began where doctors weren't calling me back. If I didn't call to check in after two or three weeks, forget it. Whatever...

I could have lain in my office for days, dead with liquid dripping out of my front door, and these doctors could have cared less. I'm serious. It was unbelievable!

Another theme also began with all of these specialists and therapists. If their Plan A didn't work, they either had no Plan B or Plan B was so messed up it was unbelievable. You'll see what I mean in a few chapters.

This was also the beginning of the testing of my perseverance. I didn't realize that this was going to end up being the greatest lesson I'd ever learn: the lesson of never giving up. It's a key ingredient to achieving what you want in life, and the more it gets ingrained in your mind, the more you will achieve.

So, if nothing else, I have that to be grateful for from this whole experience. My ability to persevere was tested and strengthened.

Doctor Worthless

Where Did You Get that Degree?

I had to figure out what this was because it was getting worse and it began affecting my life. I started to have a constant headache, although my itchy eyes had cleared up. All of my waking hours, from 6:30 in the morning to 9:30 at night, were spent in pain.

I've never had a headache problem before. I quit drinking 15 years earlier because I got really good at it (I was a binge alcoholic), and even in the days before I quit drinking, I never got headaches.

Yet now, it felt like I would wake up in the morning with someone injecting cement into my head, and it would be there for the day.

It got so bad that I started to have issues at work. I just wasn't motivated to talk to people and that was unusual for me because I'm typically a high-energy guy.

The majority of my job requires talking to people. The constant pressure in my head was just crazy. All the while, nobody besides my family knew what was happening with me. I didn't tell anybody, but everybody started to realize that there was something going on with Danny.

No matter who I saw, it seemed like all of the doctors

just thought, "Danny's got a really bad sinus infection."

At the end of 2011, I decided to go back to my general practitioner. He was a nice guy. All the women loved him because he looked like Patrick Dempsey from Grey's Anatomy. Everybody called him "Dr. McDreamy," but me? I had another nickname for him. I hate to admit it, but he didn't really help me at all. Good-looking guy, but not a good doctor.

Once the obvious diagnoses were used up, it seemed like every doctor I saw after this could only guess at what it was that I had. It was like a nightmare version of playing a game of darts. And my diagnosis was the dart board.

During the appointment, my doctor prescribed me over-the-counter stuff like Nasonex. I guess he thought I had a sinus infection since we'd ruled out an eye infection by this time.

It seems like everybody thought I had a sinus infection at this point, except for me. I was not convinced.

"Do you have a strong stomach?" he asked me.

I said, "What do you mean?"

"Can you take a lot of medicine?"

"Yeah, I'm a billy goat. I've always been. I can eat anything, drink anything, and I won't be affected."

So he told me, "Take as much Advil as you humanly can in a given day." Then he went on to add, "But don't take more than 16 pills a day."

So I started taking four Advil every four hours. It was kind of helping me a little bit, but the one thing it definitely did, lock, stock and barrel, was that it gave me my first visit with one of my many new friends on this journey: constipation.

I could not go to the bathroom for, like, a week. I'm a regular guy, too. I don't mind saying that. It was a big issue with me. I could not shit for a whole week.

I was eating cabbage, beans, coleslaw... You name it. It wasn't doing anything, but it was more important for me to get rid of my headache than the fact that I hadn't taken a dump in seven days.

I later found out that it was a really bad suggestion to have me take 16 Advil a day. Other doctors and specialists said, "Not good."

That's when I started thinking of Dr. McDreamy as "Dr. Worthless." The scary thing is, he probably graduated #104 out 105 in medical school, but that still makes him a medical doctor!

Again... Dr. Worthless.

The 2-Hour MRI

Would You Like Muzak with That?

I knew I didn't have a sinus infection and I wasn't allergic to anything, but the headaches were persisting. So, I had to continue investigating them. I went to my first Ear, Nose and Throat (ENT) doctor a few months later.

This was pretty much a waste of time. I went on a Saturday morning and she stuck a nasal scope up my nose, which was really funky. She had to numb the inside of my nose with a solution because she was sticking a big-ass wire camera up in it. That was messed up.

She looked and said, "The scope is clean. Nothing. You must have a sinus infection."

So this was Doctor #2 who said I had a sinus infection. However, because she was concerned, she said, "I want you to have an MRI."

I've had MRIs on my shoulders, knees and every part of my body, so I knew what it was. ("MRI" stands for Magnetic Resonance Imaging. It's kind of like a heavy duty x-ray).

Normally, an MRI is 20 to 45 minutes long. However, this thing took *two hours*. It was brutal.

I was locked into this enclosed tube. (If you're claustrophobic, this is a nightmare.) Then, to make matters worse, the technician asked me what type of music I wanted to hear.

I said, "Anything to make it a little upbeat. I like alternative. I can do Metallica, I can do Stones, and I like rock and roll."

This dude, for the next two hours, proceeded to play music like Air Supply and Christopher Cross. It was brutal. Just brutal.

I had to listen to elevator music for two hours sitting in an enclosed tube while being told, "Don't move."

The only thing worse was the noise of the MRI. It was just ridiculous. It was the equivalent of a drill bit for an oil rig hitting bedrock and just tearing the drill bit apart, or the yowl if you stepped on the tail of a sleeping cat.

The Pill with 97 Consonants and 2 Vowels

How Do You Spell Relief?

After the MRI, I finally went to a headache specialist.

My wife and daughters get migraines. The oldest one gets them so badly she carries meds with her for them.

I've never had migraines. I've just witnessed when they've had them and know how unpleasant they can be. So we went to a world-renowned headache clinic in Chicago.

My wife had actually been bugging me to go because she thought I had a migraine and that they could give me medicine to treat me.

At this point, I wasn't taking a lot of meds besides a gazillion Advil a day and enough laxatives to make an elephant take a dump. I was starting to shit, but only once every three days. It was horrible.

There were doctors at the headache clinic, but I didn't know if these people were really doctors, either. I think they went to the same medical school as Dr. Worthless. But, I figured somebody had to be a doctor because they prescribed me a really hardcore medication.

They looked at me and decided, "You're taking so much Advil that you're getting a headache from taking the Advil. It's called a 'rebound headache.'"

I shrugged. "Okay. I mean, I don't know, but okay."

They prescribed me a drug called Dexamethasone. Like I said, I didn't even know if these people were real doctors. They had a lot of awards and articles on their walls. They said, "Take this pill that has 97 consonants and 2 vowels. Take it twice a day. It will help."

But it didn't help at all. Nothing. Nada.

I was beginning to think to myself, *I'm a freakin' enigma!*

My wife, God bless her, always thinks she's right. She was in total shock that her Temple of Relief couldn't help me. She was like "Seriously? You're not getting better? No way!"

My body was not working and I was getting very bummed out. Work was still bad. I would go to my office and turn my light out for 8 hours and just sit at my desk. I wasn't doing anything. I work in sales and I have to talk to clients, but I was miserable. All I could do was sit at my desk and think, *Oh, this is bad.*

Things at home were getting stressful too because it's not easy living with someone who is in chronic pain.

I went about a month on the dexa-not-working drug and then the headache clinic put me on another one. I'm not even going to attempt to say it.

"It's called a cycle breaker," they said.

I asked, "What's a cycle breaker?"

They said, "Your brain is like a computer. We're going to try to reboot it completely."

A little frustrated, I said, "Why didn't we to give that to me the *first* time?"

Maybe it's my age or maybe it's my brain capacity, but I'm a person that when there's a problem with my computer, the first thing I do is turn it off and then turn it back on.

And that's what they wanted to do now. Unfortunately, it did nothing.

My wife couldn't believe it. The clinic had helped her and my daughters, but they couldn't help me.

Now I started getting really pissed off and frustrated because I was on these meds and my body was still not working. I still had a headache every single waking hour. It was relentless, from the time I woke up until the time I went to bed.

Back at work, I still wasn't really calling on clients. I spent more time on the internet looking for a solution. That's the worst thing, by the way.

If you have an ailment, throw all forms of modern technology away. Do not look at your phone or computer because you *will* mess yourself up badly. You'll start reading stuff and think, "That's what it is. That's what it is!" "It's from Indonesia." "It's the Singapore this."

You will completely mess yourself up if you look at the internet when you're sick. But of course, I did look.

What I failed to recognize was that I needed to look for support from the people I love and who love me, not the internet. I did do that later, but taking on a health issue of this nature, or any other adversity you may have in life, should not be a solitary journey.

Heads Up!

If you don't picture it,
it won't happen.

If you don't try,
it won't happen.

Guess what?

See it! Do it!

I should have leaned on the people in my life sooner. Everyone needs to. Ultimately, the answer to my problem came from sharing my experience with someone else. But I'm getting ahead of myself...

The Human Pin Cushion

Hey! That Wasn't So Bad!

Who suggested acupuncture? God, I don't know who anymore, but somebody referred me to an acupuncturist in my town.

Let me say this about her... The acupuncturist was the first specialist who truly cared about me. I could tell that she cared. My general practitioner, the eye doctor, the allergist and the headache specialists had no clue. So I decided to give the acupuncturist a try.

She tried both acupuncture and something called "cold laser treatment" on me.

Now the acupuncture was funky. She stuck little needles pretty much all over my body, like I was a human pin cushion. And I had to lay there, quietly, with needles in me for an hour. She had them in my toes and in my inner thigh. She had them everywhere.

She was really good with the acupuncture though. 99% of the time she'd put the needle in and it was fine, but there would be times where I'd feel it and she'd have to adjust the placement.

She kept putting the needles in and was going very high up on my inner thighs when I asked, "When are we stopping? We're getting to an area where I don't want a needle, please."

As she kept going, I repeated, "We're stopping. We're not going higher." Thankfully, she did!

That's when she did something real funky. This is where we got into a little bit of what seemed like carnival medicine to me. She used a procedure called "cold laser treatment." She took this *thing* and explained, "It's a laser."

I was looking for a plug to see if it was plugged in, but couldn't find one. All I knew was that it was cold and she was rubbing it all over my head and cheekbones.

Meanwhile, I was thinking to myself, *I don't know if this is a real piece of medical equipment, a toy or a prop from a movie!*

I didn't know *what* this was. It looked like something a dentist would use. But at this point, I was ready to do anything because I was in such discomfort.

The laser treatment was one of the first treatments I tried where I was thinking, "This is definitely in the world of quackery." It did not seem like a typical medical practice to me.

I went to her once a week for about a month for the needles and laser treatment. On top of that, I was still taking the meds from the headache clinic.

At that point, I was seeing multiple medical practitioners at the same time. Some doctors were saying, "That's cool. Do whatever you need to do. That's fine." Other doctors were like, "Stop doing their treatment. You've got to do my treatment or it won't work."

So at the beginning of 2012, I was receiving cross-treatment because I was desperate. If anyone said they could help me, I gave them a try.

Heads Up!

"Ladies and gentleman, we are now flying at 27,000 feet and leaving your comfort zone. You may notice a slight change in your life!"

It took a health issue to make me realize that I was going to have to leave my comfort zone and be really opened-minded. You need to take a leap of faith sometimes to get where you want to go.

The Day My Mental Health Was Questioned

Nuts! A Healthy Snack or How You're Acting?

At this point, I was going to any and every specialist to see if anyone could help me.

My opinion of Western medicine couldn't have been lower. My perspective completely changed from "These are respected physicians and medical people" to "Most of these jerks are a bunch of quacks and if their Plan A doesn't work, you're shit out of luck." That's it, because they don't have a Plan B.

After the acupuncturist, I tried an oral surgeon.

The oral surgeon was a nice guy, an older gentleman. The first thing he did was take a panoramic x-ray, which encompassed my entire mouth in one image.

He said, "Nothing is going on."

I'll say this... He was one of the first doctors to dig deep with his questions. It seemed like all of these other doctors never asked questions. They only *tell* you. They will tell you what they think and they will expound on their wealth of medical knowledge and foresight.

However, after the oral surgeon said, "I see nothing," he asked me, "Is there any stress going on in your life?"

So this was actually a big day – January 26, 2012 – the day that I began to question my own sanity. Is it possible that this was something I was causing myself?

When he said, "Is there any stress going on in your life? Maybe it's psychosomatic," I thought, *Huh. I never thought that, out of all the ailments I have, I might have a mental disorder – that I may be doing this to myself.*

From that point on, I questioned my mental state. Always. I asked every single doctor too, whether they were an oral surgeon or eye doctor, "Am I nuts?"

My head still felt like a basketball filled with cement from the time I woke up in the morning until the time I went to bed. I was taking minimal medicine, however. Taking all the Advil before freaked me out.

A friend actually said, "You know if you take too much Advil, you can have kidney failure, right?"

"Kidney failure?" I gasped.

"Yes."

So I stopped doing that.

Then I had a 3-hour exam with another eye specialist. Nothing special, kind of boring. He couldn't find anything either.

After that, I went to my second ENT doctor. This was a *highly* recommended specialist in my area, suggested by a neighbor. He said, "He's a personal friend of mine. He'll take care of you."

So I went to this guy's office for a 4pm appointment. I

got there at 3:40pm. He didn't see me until 5:30. I was so pissed off. I'm sure I must have had steam coming out of my ears. Finally, I got to see him.

Heads Up!

Tunnel vision is only good if you are *actually* in a tunnel. Look around and see everything out there!

As we looked at a CAT scan of my head, he said, "I've got to tell ya, not only do I not see anything wrong with your sinuses, you may have some of the most *perfectly* formed sinuses I have ever seen in my life."

I looked at him with disbelief and I said, "You know, that comment doesn't make me feel good, because I still have a headache."

He started to formulate something to say, but then looked at me, shrugged and said, "Yeah, I got no idea. I got nothing."

He was so dumbfounded that he couldn't even think of another specialist to send me to.

That was in February 2012. I was desperate for relief. My head was killing me and my work was suffering. One day, I just went and sat in my office and looked at the phone all day. It kept ringing but I couldn't pick it up because I couldn't talk to anybody.

I was becoming depressed. My head was killing me, my work was suffering, and my family was suffering. So

I started looking for other alternatives.

I needed to think outside the box at this point. Nothing would be too crazy and no suggestion would be too "hare-brained." When you find yourself with limited options, opening your mind to all the possibilities will only help you achieve the best solution.

Maybe You Need a Different Type of Orgasm?

Hello? Are You Listening?

Sitting in my office each day dealing with this pain, I became preoccupied with how to relax. The strain of trying to find a cure for my chronic pain while also struggling to deal with everyday life had me feeling very stressed.

I decided to get a massage. I made an appointment at the Heavenly Massage parlor, which you would think was one of those illegal places. You know, the one with the "happy ending." You wouldn't think it was therapeutic, but it was actually legit.

At Heavenly Massage, there were three older Russian ladies working the front desk and a bunch of masseuses. Every woman in there was a mildly attractive to very attractive Eastern European woman.

I made an appointment. When I went, I got in with this Russian woman who had an accent that made her sound like she just got out of the gulag.

As you know, I never told anybody in my personal life about my health problems, but as she was working on me, I started to open up a little bit. I didn't want to make my headaches my identity, but I figured she didn't know what kind of guy I usually was.

So I told her everything that was going on – that I had a headache and nobody could find the answers. What a mistake!

She proceeded to come up with everything under the sun as to what it could be and how to treat it.

The following conversation should be read in a thick Russian accent:

"Do you have any enemies?" she asked me as she rubbed my back.

I frowned a little and said, "What?"

"Enemies, enemies," she repeated.

I had to ask again to make sure I heard right. "Enemies?"

"Maybe you have enemy that put curse on you," she suggested, as serious as a heart attack.

"If that was the case, I would've had these headaches when I was 11 years old," I joked.

It didn't stop there.

"I know you're Jewish," she continued. "But even though you're Jewish, maybe you go to church and light candle. It helps. It does help."

I continued to lay there and listen to her go through her list of remedies for my headaches.

She said, "Take a combination of hot and cold

showers, real quick. Hot shower, cold shower, hot shower, cold shower."

Then she said, "Or vodka. Vodka very prominent in Russia. Helps everything. Maybe you need to drink some vodka."

Then this was the best. She said, "I know you're married man and happily married, but maybe you need different type of orgasm."

This caught me off guard. "What?"

She went on, "Maybe you need different type of orgasm to help your headache."

She then told me how she was a single mom and times were tough... I laid there and thought to myself, *Wow, I just got solicited to be a sugar daddy by a Russian masseuse.* It was classic!

Neighbors

You Can't Live with Them and OJ's Busy!

What this 2½-year odyssey taught me is that, not only are there so many different people in the world, but almost all of them have dealt with adversity of some kind at one point or another.

We need to have empathy for those around us. I learned never to judge anyone because you don't know what they are going through. I'm a case in point. For 2½ years, barely anyone knew the suffering I was enduring.

Ultimately, I believe that most people, no matter what religion, ethnicity or socioeconomic status, share a common goal. They simply want to just get through to the next day with their loved ones happy and healthy.

So if you think the Russian masseuse was the strangest person I've ever encountered, try taking a look at the people who live around me. Everyone has neighbors that annoy, irritate and just downright drive them crazy, but not everyone tells the world about them.

Let me preface by saying that these people I'm going to tell you about are hard-working good people, but absolute freaks.

Neighbor #1 - Is that a 300-Ft Antenna or Are You Just Happy to See Me?

This neighbor is a nice, quiet family with kids. The father is a ham radio enthusiast, so much that he has a special license plate stating it. (Ooh, neat!)

If I'm right, ham radio kind of went out of style around 1979 with CB radios and 8-track tape players.

About 1999, my neighbor put a 300-ft high antenna on his roof for his ham radio. I mean this thing was *huge*!

I remember calling my young daughters to come outside when he and his buddy were putting up this monstrosity and saying, "Girls, come over here. You may actually see a man fall to his death."

Forget that he can talk to people in China, he probably can talk to people on Uranus (where I'm guessing he has relatives)!

Now with cell phones and the Internet, I can't imagine this guy is using the ham radio that much anymore, but you never know.

The good news is that my house is safe during thunderstorms because I live near the world's largest lightning rod.

This neighbor is a good guy and I envy the fact that he does what he wants without caring about what anyone thinks. From what I've seen he's passed that trait on to his children, which in my eyes is a good thing.

Neighbor #2 - You Do Follow the Good Book, Don't You?

I will call these neighbors Stan and Ann. Stan and Ann are very quiet folks with two kids.

They seem nice. In 16 years, I don't think I've had a conversation longer than seven minutes with either of them though.

Tragically, Stan fell off his roof about ten years ago (shoveling snow off of it – you'd think that would be something I would do). He had serious head injuries, but is alright now (though I think ever since the fall, he believes he's Richard Nixon).

Recently in our town, there has been controversy in the high school about literature that has content that deals with homosexuality. It's gotten people in an uproar. The people that support it (my wife and myself are in that group) and super-religious folks that tend to be vehemently against it.

One day my wife, Lisa, was in our backyard and Ann approached her (probably for the first time in 16 years) and said, "Lisa, what do you think about all the stuff going on at the high school with the books?"

Lisa, not sure what to say, replied, "Ann, I really need to find out more about this before I feel comfortable taking a stance."

Nicely played. My wife definitely has a political future.

Ann replied, "Stan and I don't believe in homosexuality."

My wife stunned then says without missing a beat, "Okay... Well, you have a nice day, Ann."

As different as our outlooks on life are, I respect that these neighbors have strong beliefs (albeit sometimes misguided, I think) and I know that as people, like me, their children are their priority. Nothing pretentious about them. They live and sacrifice for their children.

Neighbor #3 - "Officer, He Seemed to Keep to Himself"

My neighbors across the street are very clean, very quiet, and very *strange*.

Dad is an older guy who is into working out, has a sports car (he washes it by hand twice a week), and works out of his home.

Mom is an extremely morose woman. (I'd say she's clinically depressed.) It looks like she has major health problems too (though I doubt she was experiencing a 24-hour/7-day-a-week headache!).

Their 33-year-old son looks like the love child of Ted Kaczynski, aka the Unibomber, and Charles Manson (long hair, goatee and, if he was any paler, he'd be see-through). He still lives at home and is unemployed after having worked for years at the local Blockbuster.

I see him sometimes leaving his house dressed in full

camouflage clothing and carrying what looks like Star Wars toys. Normal!

They do have a daughter, who my family fondly calls "Marilyn" (shout out to The Munsters). She seems really normal and nice, and is the only member of the family who has ever spoken to us in 16 years.

Marilyn is married with a baby and lives far away. (No doubt on purpose.) We see her maybe once every three years or so.

There is always someone up all night in the same room of the house with a dim light on. (I'm guessing that someone is on the computer researching how to build a bomb out of a snow blower or finding out how long it takes for a body to decompose if you bury it in your basement.) Scary!

Regardless, I don't really have any insight into the challenges they're facing, but I know that they're real enough to them as they deal with them every day. The best I can do is seek to understand them and be compassionate.

I take solace knowing that most people have neighbors who are a bit off.

Once you are able to empathize with the people around you, though something special happens. Your mind opens up, not just to the possibilities that are available to you, but to all of the solutions that are out there for you, especially in troubled times.

Heads Up!

Do not judge a person until you walk a mile in their shoes. For those of you who are out of shape, start by walking a ½ mile.

The High Priestess

Greetings from the Temple of Loony Tunes

After the first round of everything (the Russian masseuse, the allergist, the acupuncturist, the eye doctor, the ENTs, a 2-hour MRI and the headache clinic), I had gone through a series of specialists unsuccessfully. I was not getting better.

Finally, somebody told me about this woman who practiced Eastern medicine in my town. I needed relief, so I gave her a shot.

I contacted this Eastern medicine practitioner, who worked out of her home, and made an appointment to meet with her. She lived in a little split-level house in my neighborhood, actually. She was a little mousy woman who was the most earthy, holistic, cosmic, spiritual person I have ever met.

Most memorably, she was the most stone-faced human being I have ever met in my 49 years of life. I have never met anybody more serious.

If you can't tell, I like to make people laugh and I like to laugh. The second I met her, whether I was going to work with her for a day or six months, in addition to fixing my headache, my goal was to make this woman laugh. Her face only went straight across or into a frown when she was pissed with me. I wanted to see her smile.

On the first day that I met with her, I went in and she asked me a few questions. Without any kind of examination or testing, she started telling me exactly what the problem was.

"You have deep-rooted nasal congestion," she told me, even though I just had an ENT tell me I had the clearest sinuses in the history of Western Civilization.

Her response? "You have deep-rooted congestion that can't be detected by medical technology."

All I could say was, "Oh, okay."

"I can cure you. I can get rid of it," she insisted.

She was very expensive, but I decided to give her a try. So I agreed to pay her $200 an hour each week for the next three months.

During my time with the High Priestess, as I fondly called her, there were two parts to my treatment: physical and dietary.

First, I would go to her home and she would give me the physical treatments, like massaging my face and body. She would also do some real wacky stuff.

One of the wackiest things she did was hold on to bars that she had installed on her ceiling and she would walk on my stomach and my back. All the meanwhile, she never cracked a smile. She was all business.

The second part of the treatment consisted of some of the craziest shit that I ever did in this whole journey. She put me on a diet that had no gluten, sugar, red meat or dairy.

This diet sounded awfully familiar. I think it was popular in the past or maybe currently. It might be called the "No Gluten and None of the Other Crap that Kills Your Body Diet" or the "You Can't Remotely Eat Anything You Like Diet."

Then, she had a list of things she wanted me to eat in a given day. Some of it was stuff that I'd never eaten in my life – kale, this funky kind of radish, tons of protein here, this strange vegetable there. She was nuts.

The average calorie intake per day for an active male like me is between 2,400 and 2,900 calories. I was eating close to 4,000 calories a day and losing weight because I was eating stuff that was just off-the-charts freakin' healthy. There was kale, these funky milkshakes... I wasn't eating bad things, so I was losing a ton of weight.

I had never felt better in my life with the exception of my 24/7 booming headache. If I cut myself shaving, vitamin C would come out. I was that ridiculously healthy.

This was the tough part though. Every meal was a chore. My mind was constantly preoccupied with my diet. *What do I have to get for this meal? What do I have to prepare for that meal?*

It's all I thought about all day. Then, each meal was huge – ginormous meals full of vegetables and protein. It would take me forever to eat each one.

But the *worst* part was that she would change my diet *daily* or every other day. Two days into it, she'd be like, "Take this out. Add this." She did that almost every single day.

One time, she changed my diet twice in one day. "You're driving me shithouse crazy," I exclaimed. "I can't live like this! You're driving me nuts!"

She genuinely tried to help me, but I wasn't getting anywhere with her. I thought she would be "it," because she had convinced me that her prognosis was "it," but she was nuts. I thought she was certifiably crazy. Little did I know at the time that she'd come the closest to the answer of anyone I'd seen thus far.

I felt healthier than I ever had before, but my headaches were still bad. I decided to look somewhere else because I just couldn't continue to live with these headaches.

By this time, I had had the satisfaction of finally making her laugh. (I don't remember what I said, but I do know I made her laugh.)

So finally I told her, "High Priestess, it's not working. I have to go in a different direction, but I appreciate everything you've done."

Then I said to her, "You're only the second person who genuinely cared about me throughout this whole process. Thank you for that."

Sometimes when we're in the midst of adversity, it's easy to forget to say "thank you," but recognizing the contribution of others is important, both to our own progress as well as to them.

Plan B

Living the Life of a Super Model

After I stopped seeing the High Priestess, nothing much really happened. I was still taking aspirin or Tylenol, but no heavy-duty meds.

Then, somebody told me about this neurologist who was one of the foremost headache specialists in the country... *and he's in my town!* They said he was very difficult to get in with, but he was absolutely the best practitioner around.

All I could say was, "I'm going!"

So I set up an appointment with this guy. As I walked into the waiting room, the first thing I noticed were the walls. His waiting room walls were covered in pictures of him winning awards. On the coffee tables, there were magazines with his name on them and post-it notes that said where his articles were published.

You gotta be kidding me. Who does this guy think he is? Albert Einstein? Sigmund Freud?

I finally got called in and I met him. He was this sawed-off, little nerdy guy. I sat there and waited for him to ask me my name, but the first thing he started doing was to hand me a photocopy of an article. I looked at it and discovered that it was an article he had written, of course. I was still waiting for this guy to talk to me, but he proceeded to hand me another article. And another. And another.

He proceeded to hand me *six* articles.

As he went to grab #7, I said, "Doctor, with all due respect, you can stop handing me these sheets of paper. I'm not reading *any* of them!"

He sat back and had a look on his face that read, *Oh my God!* because, I guessed, his other patients have bowed down to him and kissed his ring. *Sorry dude, you put your pants on one leg at a time like me and I'm not that impressed.*

I said, "I'm coming to *you*. You were referred to me not only as an expert, but as one of the best people in this field. I need to hear from you. I need you to tell me what to do for my specific situation."

So he started telling me all this crap about headaches and stuff like that.

"My #1 treatment with the best rate of success is Botox injections."

"Botox injections?" I repeated in astonishment.

"Yes," he said. "We have a Botox injection treatment and *that's* what works. That is *absolutely* what will work."

So I agreed to try it.

I had to fill out all these forms and wait for three

weeks for my appointment. I wasn't really excited. I am not a big lover of needles. I mean, I'm not scared of pain and have a high threshold for it, but getting a shot in the head really didn't excite me.

Finally, I went to get the injections. He wasn't even the one who did it. He had an assistant do it. She gave me *18 shots* in my face and head.

Let's put it this way... It was not pleasant, not remotely pleasant. I only did it because it was supposedly this guy's thing – his expertise.

The assistant said it would take about ten days before I would be feeling some relief. Then they would do another evaluation to see if I needed a second treatment.

So I got home, but not only was it not getting better – *it started feeling worse!* I just took 18 injections in my head and my headaches were getting worse. By day five, I told my wife, "I've got to call this guy. This is bad."

I picked up my phone and said, "Doc, not only didn't the shots help, but it's worse! I'm in some *serious* pain right now!"

There was a short pause until he finally said, "Well... You know that's really, really odd because I have about an 85% success ratio on this kind of treatment."

In steaming exasperation I replied, "I apologize for screwing up your *numbers,* but my head is fucking *killing* me!"

He paused again, as if he didn't know what to say, and then finally spoke. "I think maybe we should go this route," he began. "Why don't you start taking two Advil in the morning and two Advil before you go to bed?"

I wanted to kill this guy. I could not believe he just said that. It was unbelievable. I said, "Are you *serious*, Doctor? Plan B is getting over-the-counter pain relievers? Do you not think that in the year and a half that I've been suffering, maybe I haven't taken a couple of pain relievers? Please tell me this is *not* Plan B."

There was silence in my ear. He said nothing. I hung up because I was completely flabbergasted. All I could think was, *I cannot freakin'...*

I was ready to get in my car and drive to that guy's office so I could rip his head off his shoulders, but I called my wife instead and she calmed me down.

You're going to meet a lot of different people in your life and some won't be too nice. Some might be downright awful! But always strive for empathy. We all have a common goal at the end of the day... And we're each in pursuit of that goal. It doesn't matter if you live in New York City or on a mountain in Nepal, everyone just wants to get to the next day with their loved ones and themselves healthy and happy.

The Hall of Fame of Side Effects

If Crazy is Relative, This is a Family Reunion!

After I calmed down from dealing with the headache specialist who told me take Advil, one of my wife's closest friends referred me to her sister-in-law, who is a rheumatologist.

A rheumatologist deals with autoimmune diseases and joints, stuff like that. They aren't orthopedic, but they do a whole lot of related things.

What was interesting about this lady is that she was doctor #3 who actually cared about me. There was no doubt about it. She absolutely cared about me. In fact, she was more like a therapist than a doctor because I could tell her how I was feeling emotionally, not just physically. To her, I wasn't a walking collection of symptoms, a problem to be solved. I was a living, breathing human being, and I knew she saw me that way.

She was so caring and concerned. It was such a nice change of pace after going to Dr. Frankenputz, to go to somebody like her. She was the doctor in the practice who is essentially the medical detective. She researches the wacked-out stuff, not just issues related to autoimmune diseases. If there's a mystery illness, she's the one who finds out about it. She was an open-minded person, the kind that would "go out there."

She told me, "I don't know what it is you have," which was nice because she was probably the 5ᵗʰ doctor out of 20 who said, "I'll take the zero. I have no idea what you have," rather than the ones who were like, "Yes, it's this. My treatment will work and if it doesn't work, you've never heard of me. You've never seen me. You were never a patient of mine." At least she was honest.

She actually said flat-out, "I don't know what this is, but let's see if we can manage the pain."

"Fine," I said.

Now this is where there was a bit of déjà vu. She was a doctor, so obviously she could prescribe almost any drug she wanted. She said, "I'm going to try to reboot your brain like you'd reboot a computer." (Where had I heard *that* before?)

I said, "Well, I turn mine off when I do that."

"We're not gonna go that far," she explained. "But I'm going to be reboot the computer in your head." She took out a prescription pad and said, "What are your thoughts on taking medicine?"

"I'll take the experimental stuff that they won't give to *mental* patients. I'll take *anything*," I pleaded. "I just want to get rid of these headaches."

"Okay," she nodded. Then she began to write out a prescription. She handed me the blue prescription paper with a handwritten note and told me to take it to the pharmacy. I brought the note closer to me and read it.

It said, "Please prescribe this pill and this pill. Now, I realize that the combination of taking both pills at the same time could kill him, but please let him take them."

I was like, "Oh my God! What are you giving me?"

She said to me, "This is going to hopefully manage your pain, but let me tell you what the side effects could be."

That was nice, really nice, of her, I thought. I've had doctors in this 2½-year journey that didn't tell me a thing about any potential side effects of the drugs I was taking. How bad is that? Total quacks.

"There are really five possible side effects," she continued. She began listing them. "Short-term memory loss, moodiness, lack of energy, constipation and equipment failure" (down below, which by the way is really demoralizing for a male).

The constipation was the cherry on top of the side-effect sundae. "You may have one of them," she said. "I've heard of people experiencing two, which is rare, but you'll probably only just have one if you have any."

It turned out that she gave me heavy duty brain stabilizers that were some of the *strongest* meds – actually, they *were* the strongest meds – that I've ever been on in my life.

Remember those five side effects, even though I was only supposed to experience one? Well, it turned out that I got into the Hall of Fame for side effects because I had *all* of them. I took two pills that completely shut my body off. It made me like the walking dead. I was a zombie. I was functioning like I was on life support, but I was moving around.

First, the short-term memory loss began. I couldn't remember any of my phone conversations. I had to write down every conversation I had with a client because I couldn't remember it after I was done.

Then, there was the moodiness. I had two moods with these pills, depression and anger. Those were my moods.

Next of course we had constipation, nothing good about carrying that around and not letting it out. I was trying anything to get things going again, eating meals of cabbage, chili and prunes with a side of baked beans. Nothing.

All that accomplished was tremendous amounts of gas or DBABs (Deadly Brown Air Biscuits), which did not make me the most popular guy in the house living with my three women.

I would sit on the toilet for hours at a time with nothing happening (besides reading every magazine that was in my house, including Cosmo) and actually thinking, *This is going to kill me.* My thoughts jumped to "Gosh, I hope the girls don't call the new guy 'Dad?'"

As I near the advanced age of 50, I've realized that there are two things that are imperative in my life: a good night's sleep and being able to take a dump on a regular basis.

Time for "Personal Meds"

Inspiration is the Love Child of Desperation and a Serious *#@%$# Headache!

That brings us to the Fall of 2013 when I was probably at the lowest time of my life. My chronic daily headaches had not only taken over my life, but they were ruining it.

Everything was bad. My work was bad, my marriage was bad, my family life was bad, and I really wasn't good for much of anyone or anything. I was on meds that made me a zombie who couldn't remember a thing. I had no energy, couldn't take a dump, and my man equipment was on total shutdown.

My life spiraled downward and though I never thought of taking my life, there were times where I actually thought, *You know, if I go to bed tonight and don't wake up tomorrow morning, I'm okay with that.*

I knew I had enough life insurance that my family would be okay and they wouldn't have to deal with me being so miserable and depressed. I knew too that they wouldn't consider my death to be a good thing, but that's where I was mentally.

Finally, I had an idea that might give me some relief from my misery. Smoking marijuana – pot, weed, herb, ganja or whatever you want to call it. I'd smoked in college and occasionally socially after that, but I had pretty much stopped after I had my first daughter.

When I quit drinking in 1999, I also vowed to never smoke pot or take any substance that could alter me or that I could get addicted to. These were desperate times though and I was as desperate as I had ever been in my life. So I approached my wife with the idea, knowing that if she didn't sign off on it, I wouldn't pursue it.

She said to me "How can I say no?" That's why I love this woman so much!

So now I was on a mission. Where could I get it? I guess I could go to the high school around lunch time and get some. Not really funny, but sadly true.

No, I was going to have to go the grown-up route to get my illegal contraband.

After talking to a few folks (you wouldn't believe how many suburbanites in their 40s smoke pot), I found a fellow who could help me out. He was an avid pot smoker and said he would be more than happy to help, especially knowing that this was truly going to be for medicinal purposes.

Now since I was trying to be careful (as careful as you can be buying an uncontrolled illegal substance) and having not bought pot in over 25 years, I asked my friend, "So is this pot good?"

He said, "Danny, I make a lot of money and I'm a drug addict. It's the best!"

Good enough for me. He got my seal of approval. So the next time I saw him, he gave me a bag that had a bag inside it that had another bag inside it and then an old prescription bottle. I appreciated him being cautious, but holy fucking moly! This was like having to go through four nesting dolls to get the contraband.

He then said to me, "Danny, this isn't pot from the '70s or '80s. It's one-hit pot. You take one hit and you're good for three hours."

So we concluded our illicit transaction and went our separate ways.

I got home and had some planning to do. I live with two teenage daughters who have been told that even though their Mom and Dad believe marijuana should be legal, it is not and they are not to do it. So I had to figure out where to hide it and when to do it.

Based on the fact that my daughters have a phobia of working out and exercising, I hid my new "personal meds" in a pair of rollerblades that had been collecting dust for the last ten years. Lighter and pipe in one skate, personal meds in other.

Now it was time to take a test drive. I chose a night

when my wife and the girls would be out. I thought it would be best if they weren't around, especially if I had a bad reaction, like passing out drooling or having a full-body seizure.

I lit the pipe and took a long drag. It had been a long time and I immediately started coughing as if I had just been injected with a strain of the whooping cough virus.

After I got done almost coughing my left lung out, I sat down and felt the effects immediately. My friend wasn't lying. This pot was strong. I was high as a kite, on one hit, mind you. One hit and I was as high as I had ever been in my life.

Here was the good news. It didn't take my headache away, but it was the first time in about 18 months that I felt kind of good. The pain wasn't gone, but it definitely took it from a pain level of 10 down to a 5.

Hey, at that point, I was willing to take any small victory I could get. I started getting high almost nightly, but didn't do it during the day. I also never did it in front of my kids, and I never drove cars high or assembled any type of furniture from IKEA.

There was one drawback to this that wasn't terrible, but wasn't good either. Not every time, but often enough, when I got high I would get a bad case of the munchies (really hungry for you non-drug addicts). Even though

I'm 5'7" and 160lbs, I already eat like a guy who is 6'3" and 250lbs, and now add being stoned. Not good. I was walking into my kitchen like I did as a 15-year-old scouring the fridge and pantry to see what I could eat. Ice cream, potato chips, popcorn, salami sandwiches, frozen pizzas, whatever I could find.

Heads Up!

Tough situations are like in-laws. You better figure out a solution to dealing with them because they're not going away for a long time!

Luckily, my teenage daughters were fairly self-absorbed and never really commented on the fact that Dad was putting away about 5,000 calories every other night or so.

I'm not proud that I resorted to taking an illegal drug, but it really helped. It also made me realize that marijuana for medicinal purposes can be beneficial. (It probably didn't hurt the economy either. I loved the Cheetos and microwave burritos from the local convenience store!)

When you are in chronic pain, you'll eat goat shit to feel better. I know smoking pot gave me a little bit of much-needed relief in my journey through Hell.

I truly feel in my heart that marijuana should be legal, at least for medicinal purposes. People in chronic pain aren't using it for fun or just to get high. They're using it to make it through the day without pain or so they can eat more because the meds they are taking decrease their appetite.

This should not be looked upon as morally or ethically wrong. Quite the opposite. It's a blessing and it's natural. It should be available to anyone who is suffering and just trying to make it through the day with their loved ones.

The Last Resort...?

Not a Great Time to Be Cheap

At this point, I was still plagued with the five side effects brought on by the medication I was taking, but most of all I was dealing with severe constipation. I was taking enough laxatives to make a circus elephant take a dump. Yet I still couldn't. It was unbelievable. I even took stuff they gave livestock to shit and I couldn't. How messed up is that?

The final side effect I suffered from was "equipment failure." (Not "equipment not working great," not "some days good, some days not so good"). It was in a complete shutdown. My privates were in a coma and that messes you up as a man.

I'm not that old and I like to think that I'm still sexually active, but it was in a complete shutdown. From the age 12 or 13 on, it's a guy's best friend... So when that friend is in a coma, you're bumming out. It's incredibly demoralizing.

I was going insane amidst these side effects. I went to work, but I didn't call any clients because I was terrified of what I was going to say to people.

I was as irritated as calling the cable company with a simple question about my service. I was essentially living in a body with a non-functioning brain, frustrated all the time. I saw what was going on, but I couldn't control anything. It was like I was under anesthetic, but I was awake.

Still, I tried to do everything that I normally did in life because I was never going to let this illness define me.

I was playing basketball, which I used to keep up with for two hours straight. But now, I was gassed after ten minutes. I had no energy.

Nobody I played with knew about my headaches so everybody was like, "*What* is wrong with you? You're typically the Energizer Bunny and after 10 minutes you're gassed?"

Not wanting to become "the guy with the headaches," I simply told them I was out of shape. It was brutal. I almost quit and, you can ask my wife, playing my pickup basketball game is the love of my life. I lived like this for the next six or seven months and it was unbelievably trying.

The headaches were lessened, but they didn't go away completely and my whole body, including my brain, was a walking state of utter numbness.

The rheumatologist I was seeing was the sweetest doctor. She was great. She kept encouraging me, but I finally told her that I would have to try something else. This was when I started to wean myself off the meds she had me on.

Eventually, I talked to my dentist. I love my dentist. He is like the father I never had. He kept telling me, "You've got to go to the Mayo Clinic. You've got to go to the Mayo Clinic. They *are the best*."

So finally, with pretty much no other options, I decided to go to the Mayo Clinic. It was wild. When people hear "the Mayo Clinic" – at least when I heard it – they think it's the *last* resort. It's the place where people go because the doctors there are the best in the world and you're clutching your last straw.

I mean, people fly in... Dignitaries, presidents, everybody, because it's the best medical facility in the world.

At this point, everything in my life was still bad. My work was bad. My marriage was bad. I wasn't being good to my kids. I was in chronic friggin' pain, my man parts weren't working and I was depressed. I finally said, "I've got to go to the Mayo Clinic. I've got to see what these kids think."

I made an appointment and I planned on being there for a week. It didn't seem that long, so stupid me, when I booked a room, I was cheap. I went for price and I shouldn't have.

I got to the hotel and it was a *dump*. It was a *bad* hotel. There was a paper floor mat in the bathroom and a chain lock for the door. Just looking at the bedsheets made me fearful. God knows what was on there. It was bad, really bad, and I was already feeling bad.

The fact that I was at the Mayo Clinic made me think *I am either extremely sick and I don't know it or I am insane.* If I was betting, insane verses terminally ill, I would have gone for insane.

I did not want to be in that hotel. It was sad, too, because there were families there and it was probably all they could afford.

Heads Up!

Listen to your gut. It's the best internal compass you will ever have and it's also a great place to store beer and pizza!

Luckily, I was able to switch hotels and I moved to a Courtyard Marriott that was connected to the hospital, which was better because it was the middle of February in Rochester, Minnesota, and it was cold, snowy and freezing.

The Village of Desperation

A Smile is a Frown Turned Upside Down

The Mayo Clinic is absolutely the most impressive and depressing medical facility that I have ever seen in my life.

It was impressive because everything was fluid. For example, you'd see a doctor at 10:00am. He would check you, and then you would have an appointment with another doctor at 4:00pm. That doctor would have all the stuff that just got checked by the first doctor. It was very fluid. Everything was flowing.

By the way, I saw a lot of people who were way worse off than me. There were people and children in bad physical shape. It was brutal. Let's put it this way... If you see somebody at the Mayo Clinic, you don't ask, "How are you doing?" How do you think I'm doing? I'm at the Mayo Clinic!

So I went to the first doctor I was scheduled to see. He was a young guy. He checked me out and asked me a gazillion questions. He started out with the basic health questions and then started asking me 21 more.

"How many times do you masturbate?"

"How many hours do you work?"

"How many cigars have you smoked in your life?"

And every other question known to man. I respected him for it, compared to some of those other doctors I had seen, but it took us at least two hours.

After that, I had to get a blood test. This part was crazy. My appointment was at 10:45 the next morning. They told me where to go and I walked into a 10,000 square foot open area with four doors. All it was, were people constantly getting their blood taken. I sat down and waited for them to call my name as I watched people endlessly walk in and walk out.

Finally, they called, "Friedman, Door 3."

I got up and went through Door 3. I sat down in the chair and the tech began wrapping my arm and taking my blood. I asked curiously, "How many people do you guys see on a given day?"

"1,200," the tech casually replied.

"Oh my God," I gasped. 1,200 people a day get their blood drawn! It was the Village of Desperation! 6,000 people getting their blood taken every week in that one facility. That's a lot of sickness. It was unreal.

On the third day of my stay at the Village of Desperation, I was seeing this neurologist. I was waiting in the room, looking at her diplomas from the University of I'm Smarter than Anybody You've Ever Met in Your Life, when suddenly this woman with really bad bedside manners walked in. She was *not* pleasant.

The first doctor I saw, the young guy... He was nice and compassionate. He had feelings. This woman? She was a robot. She wasn't warm at all and warmth was what I needed at that time.

She spent the next ten minutes reviewing my information, looking at all my stuff and then she started shaking her head. Never once did she ask me a question or acknowledge my presence in the room. I was sitting on the bench starting to well up as I sat right next to her and watched, waiting for her verdict.

Finally, she said, "I've got to tell you, I don't see a thing. Not only are you fit, but you're *really* fit for your age."

That's when I lost it. I completely broke down and started crying like a baby. I could feel the hot tears build up in my eyes and then smoothly glide down my face.

"Am I crazy?" I asked in between my tears. "Is this psychosomatic? Am I insane? Do I need to see a psychiatrist?"

It felt like all hope was lost and my heart just sank. "You *can't* tell me that you can't find anything. There's *no* way I've had headaches for two years for no reason. You *can't* tell me that. I'm at the *Mayo Clinic!*"

It took her a moment to respond as she gathered her

thoughts. There was no reaction to the display of human emotion right there in front of her.

Slowly, she began, "Well, there's one other guy. He's the best headache specialist at the Mayo Clinic. He really is the best."

She agreed to look into it for me. I sat back down and she made a couple of phone calls. After a few minutes, she hung up and said, "We can probably get you in by May."

My eyes widened. "May?" I repeated. "That's two months from now! I'm gonna kill myself! May?"

Sighing, she replied, "Hold on," before leaving the office.

I stayed behind and kept crying my eyes out. I began thinking to myself, *There's nothing wrong with me. I'm crazy. The best person they've got can't see me for two months. I can't make it for that long. I'm not going home. I can't make it for two more months.*

After what felt like an eternity, the door opened and the doctor returned. "It's your lucky day," she smiled. "You can see him tomorrow morning at 9am."

My tears suddenly stopped flowing and my heart momentarily lit up. Finally, another ray of hope. I was almost going to kiss that woman, but then I thought she might melt like the Wicked Witch of the West if I touched her with any of my emotion.

It was another ray of hope, but I was still in bad shape mentally and emotionally. I remember it so well. It was a Thursday night. My wife was scared to the point that she was going to fly out to be with me. I sounded *that* bad.

I didn't want to talk to anybody. My phone kept ringing. Every time I picked it up and looked at who it was, it would be my mother or my siblings. But I didn't want to talk to anybody. It was the lowest I had ever been in my life. When the Mayo Clinic said, "We don't see anything," I thought to myself, *I am one crazy dude. I am shithouse nuts.*

Eventually, I fell asleep. I woke up the next day and got ready to go see this doctor and hoped for some kind of answer. I opened the door to his room and took a seat. As I waited, I looked at the diplomas on his walls that said University of Smarter than that Broad You Saw Yesterday. So I thought to myself, *Good! He's smart.*

Finally, he came in and introduced himself. He began looking at my chart, just like every other doctor had.

I said, "Doc, have you ever seen anything like this?"

"About five times a day," he replied as he flipped through my file.

"You're kidding me," I gasped in astonishment.

Now, he couldn't come up with a concrete answer of what it was, but he basically said, "I've got the meds that have worked for most of my headache patients. It's going to a take a month or two, but they should work."

I was so happy. I went from wanting to kill myself to ecstatic within 24 hours. I was so relieved that I wanted to kiss the guy on the mouth, hug him or buy him a new car. Finally, somebody to whom my illness was not a mystery. He said, "I've seen this a lot and know how to treat it."

By the time I left the Mayo Clinic, I was very optimistic. I was feeling good. He ended up putting me on a very strong medication. It wasn't as strong as the pills from the rheumatologist, but it was still very strong.

I didn't suffer from the same side effects of the earlier drugs, but it was still slowing me down. My body stopped working again... I wasn't digging it, but I had no other choice than to stick with it. The drive to find a cure for my headaches led me to do and try things I would have thought crazy before. If I needed to stick with these meds for a while longer, that was exactly what I was going to do. Simply put, I'm not a quitter. I was going to beat this thing, come Hell or high water.

Within the next two months or so, I was actually beginning to experience some good days along with the bad. It was like being on a roller coaster.

I stayed on the meds from the Mayo Clinic for a total of six months. I wasn't happy, but I wasn't losing my mind. I was certainly feeling a little bit of relief.

The medications were still strong enough to mess me up, though. They still slowed me down. Even though I had some good days, I still felt like I was in limbo.

I was learning how to manage this, how to live with the headaches. But that's not what I wanted! I had no intention of stopping until I got rid of them.

Heads Up!

Positives are like sunrises. There's at least one every day!

It seemed like 95% of all the specialists and doctors I went too said, "Our goal is to manage it," and I didn't agree with them. I said *Fine. That's your goal, but my goal is to get rid of this.*

I am a goal-oriented person. I set goals and I achieve them. I always have. And my goal now was to get rid of this. I didn't want to manage it. I didn't want to be medicated. I wanted to be cured.

Perseverance was going to be needed now more than ever. I'd come this far and giving up was not an option. I was never going to give up. I was not going to succumb to my headache. I was going to beat this.

The Final A-Ha

The Road to Success Starts with a Really Good Map!

A few months after I visited the Mayo Clinic, I was still on the meds they'd prescribed, but I knew I needed to do something instead. I didn't know what, but I was definitely going to wean myself off these drugs.

I decided that, if I was going to be in pain, I wanted to do it in my own body. It was taxing, but I started to wean myself off them.

That summer, I started talking to a client of mine, a woman whose account had grown with me. Since we kept working on projects together, I started talking to her and opening up more each week as we got to know one another better. At one point, we started talking about personal stuff.

One day, out of the blue, she said, "I had chronic headaches for a year."

"You're kidding me!" I gasped, immediately interested in her story.

"No," she shook her head.

"I'm *living* through chronic headaches," I confessed.

"I don't have them anymore," she revealed.

"What do you mean you don't have them anymore?"

"I went to a doctor out by me," she began. My client

lives in a city about an hour away from where I live, so her doctor was pretty far, but that was fine with me. Listen, I would have driven to Siberia to get my head fixed.

"She's an osteopath," she continued.

"What's an osteopath?" I learned that an osteopath is a person who is one-third a doctor with seven years of medical training, one-third a chiropractor, and one-third homeopath. I'm in!

"Did they ever find out how you got the headaches?" I asked her.

"They think it started when I had a tooth pulled and an implant put in."

Heads Up!

Mix it up! Do something that would make a sane person say, "Why'd they do that?" Then do it until they say, "Wow! Now I know why they did that!" or "Why didn't I think of that?"

"No way," I cried. She nodded her head.

"Oh my God," I continued to say in awe, "Oh my God, that's it!"

It was the a-ha moment. That was *it*. A year before I started getting headaches, I had a tooth pulled and an implant put in!

That was *it*. I almost started to cry.

"Are you telling me the truth?" I demanded to know, ready to have a happy breakdown.

She said, "Yes."

"I have to see your doctor. I have to see her. I have to see her *today!*"

They Saved My Life

All Systems Go!

I was so happy to finally hear something that made sense – the tooth that I had pulled and the implant that was put in. When I got the tooth pulled, it was the first time I ever went through something like that. I was 46 or 47 at the time.

The whole process was like an episode from the Three Stooges. The oral surgeon put his pliers on the tooth, he put his foot on the chair, and he started yanking. He used anesthetic on it, but I was awake the whole time and he was just yanking away. Getting a tooth pulled is a violent act.

I made an appointment with the osteopath and she turned out to be this nice woman, about 60 years old, and from what I could tell she was an extremely compassionate person.

During my first appointment, I told her my story and what my client had told me about her. She was like, "Yeah, it's the pulled tooth. No question. Your skull shifted."

She proceeded to show me two holes on this skeleton head. "There are two holes at the bottom of your skull that cerebral fluid and congestion flow out of," she explained. "Yours got shifted when your oral surgeon pulled your tooth out and now everything is blocked up in your head."

All I could think was, *That makes sense!*

I asked her what her goal was with me.

She answered, "To get rid of your headaches completely"

Eureka! Not managing the pain, not making me feel a bit better, but curing me. I was in heaven.

I agreed to let her do a procedure on me that was a chiropractic alignment. The first time I went to get the alignment done, the woman asked me if it was okay if she said a prayer.

"I don't care if you rub a dead chicken on me," I said. "Whatever you want to do, do it! If you want me to get naked I will because vanity went out the window two years ago."

She said her prayer and ended with "amen." I'm not even religious and I said, "Amen," too.

Then she began to treat me.

If you've ever been to a chiropractor, you know they do some funky maneuvers to get your body aligned. Lots of pulling, bending and yanking of body parts. Well, she was doing this stuff and then she did something that scared the shit out of me. (Where was she when I didn't have a bowel movement for five months?)

She said, "Hang your head over the table and I'm going to crack your neck."

Uh, pardon me? Crack my neck?

I thought, *Maybe she's planning to fix my headaches by breaking my neck. Being paralyzed will certainly distract me from my headaches.*

So I said, "Uh... Okay?"

She pulled on my neck and it made a sound so horrific that all I could think was, *At least I'm going to get great parking spots from now on.*

It not only was fine, but I felt better.

She then started doing something called "craniosacral therapy." It was the most bizarre thing. She was barely touching my head, but she was manipulating my skull. She put her fingers in my mouth and did stuff to it. I *instantly* started to feel relief.

We did this for the next seven months. There was nothing traditionally medical to it and, at this point, I was completely weaned off my meds.

I started to get my old energy back, which was nice. I was mentally sharp, which made work so much easier. I was pooping on a regular basis, which made me much more pleasant for my girls to be around. And my libido was back, which my wife really enjoyed.

Getting off all of my meds after two years was unbelievable. I began to have good days. Days with no headaches. After I was completely weaned off the meds, I was so jacked up from feeling good that I didn't sleep for *five days*!

I felt like a total meth addict! I had so much energy that it was a joke. I was playing basketball again without getting gassed out after ten minutes.

I started to go to the osteopath weekly, which also included seeing her assistant when she was too busy. The assistant was also trained in craniosacral therapy.

They cured me. They *cured* me. It took seven months of weekly visits, but they *cured* me.

Finally, after two years and eight months, I was well again. I bought them a big-ass mountain of chocolate for Christmas. It was enough to give every staff member in that office diabetes.

Heads Up!

Try new things. If we never tried new things, you'd be reading this on a cave wall.

I told the osteopath and her assistant, "You saved my life."

I told the client who referred me, "You saved my life."

And I don't say it lightly.

They saved my life. They saved my family.

Once Again, Never Give Up

I Think I Can, I Think I Can, I Know I Can!

Ever since this ordeal ended, I've said to people, "You've seen on CNN when a guy goes into a shopping mall and shoots up the place because he went off his meds. It's tragic when that happens. If the guy was on his meds, he probably wouldn't have done that. I can empathize with them though, not for their actions, but for the fact that some people do not want to be medicated."

The whole experience is horrible. You no longer feel human when you're medicated. More times than not, you're like somebody with Alzheimer's. Sometimes you're in, sometimes you're out, and it's just frustrating because your brain is not working.

In my scenario, it was my brain and my body that was not working.

You know how everybody says, "Health is everything?"

That's lip service. Even I used to say, "health is everything." It's bullshit. Until you go through something horrible, some chronic pain, an illness, chronic depression... Until you go through something that debilitates and changes your life, you don't know squat.

I would have given away all my worldly possessions, including my money and my home, to get better. That's how miserable my life was. These people? They saved my life.

I still go for tune-ups every once in awhile, but I am completely headache free two years later.

I kept my headaches a secret for two and a half years because I didn't want to become the poster child for headaches. But I am ready to talk with people about it now, especially people who are in chronic pain.

A lot of what I've learned during this time can be applied to other kinds of adversity. It doesn't matter whether you're dealing with overwhelming debt, a failing marriage, or a health condition.

I never allowed my headaches to become my identity. I want people to learn how to apply the same mindset and determination that I did.

I want to encourage you to never give up. Never, ever give up.

Heads Up!

Live the 3 Ps!

Positive (Be Positive!),

Prepared (Plan and write down goals) and

Practice (work your plan and never give up until you achieve your goal)

And if you're up to it, live the 4th P,

Pie! (Who doesn't like pie?)

About the Author

Danny Friedman is a multimillion-dollar sales professional with over 25 years of experience. He has achieved success in the office equipment, commercial real estate, sporting goods and promotional products industries.

In 2007, Danny started DANNY, Inc., a sales training company that features Danny's highly energized style of speaking. He is not only educational, but inspirational.

Danny is recognized as an expert in the world of sales and his sessions are a "must see." His pragmatic style delivers a winning message to each one of his audiences, whether there are 25 or 1,000 people.

He speaks at national association tradeshows as well as corporate functions and is in demand both domestically and internationally.

Danny speaks to schools, healthcare organizations and corporations about his life and what he has overcome to inspire others to do the same. His sessions will make you laugh, cry and inspire you "to never give up," no matter what battle you are dealing with.

Audiences learn of the many treatments, physicians and alternative medical practices Danny endured until he finally found the solution to overcome his personal nightmare.

Danny's audiences leave with the inspiration to succeed in their personal life. It is his belief that everyone is entitled to live a happy and healthy life.

Danny lives in Chicago with his wife and 2 daughters.

Learn more about the author at dannyinc.com.

CPSIA information can be obtained
at www.ICGtesting.com
Printed in the USA
FFOW05n0759280515

9 780692 397367